DIY

Debt Elimination

The Only True Guide You Will Ever Need To Creating A Budget

© 2011 MoneyGuy77.com

Legal

Limit of Liability and Disclaimer of Warranty:

The publisher has used its best efforts in preparing this book, and the information provided herein is provided "as is." MoneyGuy77.Com makes no representation or warranties with respect to the accuracy or completeness of the contents of this book and specifically disclaims any implied warranties of merchantability or fitness for any particular purpose and shall in no event be liable for any loss of profit or any other personal or commercial damage, including but not limited to special, incidental, consequential, or other damages.

Trademarks:

This book identifies product names and services known to be trademarks, registered trademarks, or service marks of their respective holders. They are used throughout this book in an editorial fashion only. In addition, terms suspected of being trademarks, registered trademarks, or service marks have been appropriately capitalized, although MoneyGuy77.Com cannot attest to the accuracy of this information. Use of a term in this book should not be regarded as affecting the validity of any trademark, registered trademark, or service mark. MoneyGuy77.Com is not associated with any product or vendor mentioned in this book

Sharing this Document :

The information in this document is copyrighted. I would ask that you do not share this information with others, you purchased this book, and you have a right to use it for yourself. Another person who has not purchased this book does not have that right. It is the sales of this valuable information that makes the continued publishing of MoneyGuy77.Com possible. If enough people disregard that simple economic fact, these books or website will no longer be viable or available.

It should go without saying that you cannot post this document or the information it contains on any electronic bulletin board, Web site, FTP site, newsgroup, or ... well, you get the idea. The only place from which this document should be available is from the MoneyGuy77.Com Web site or designated vendors.
 Finally, nothing in this guide is intended to replace common sense, legal, medical or other professional advice, and is meant to inform and entertain the reader.

Table Of Contents

Chapter 1

Calculating Your Total Debt

The very first step, in the elimination of debt , is to determine exactly how much you owe. In order to understand this equation you will need to do some basic math. Take out a piece of paper and list all your bills from your highest bill to your lowest. You can use the table below as a format for your Debt to Income ratio calculations.

Example:

List Of Monthly Bills		Monthly Income	
Mortgage (PITI)/ Rent	$	Income 1	$
Car Payment(s)	$	Income 2	$
Car Insurance	$	Income 3	$
Credit Card(s) (Minimum's)	$		
Student Loans	$		
Child Support	$		
Misc Loan(s) (Minimum)	$		
Cell Phone	$		
Utilities (Water,Electricity)	$		
Any Other Monthly Debt	$		
Total	$	Total	$

Once you list all your debt then you will need to total the amount at the bottom of the page. The next step is to determine your income. Many financial institutions calculate your Debt to Income ratio using your gross pay and subtract the taxes out of the gross in order to get your adjusted gross net income.

This is very similar to the way you input the information in a 1040 form. However, for this instance, you will need to use your net income (after taxes) or what you are actually bringing home.

After you have listed your income then you will need to list any additional income you have such as a side job, bonuses (if these are quarterly or yearly you will need to divide the amount by 4 or 12 to get a monthly figure) then write these figures down. After you have written down all income now you will need to total the income at the bottom of your worksheet.

Now that you have both figures totaled at the bottom of your worksheet. You will now take the figures and divide your total income into your total debt.

Example:

Total Income	$ 6000.00
Total Debt	$ 2000.00
Total Debt To Income Ratio	33%

If your total income for the month was $6000.00 dollars. And, your debt was $2000.00 dollars. Then divide the $6000.00 into the $2000.00 which would give you a 33% debit to income ratio...

Now that you know your actual debt to income ratio you may ask why this factor is so important ? When you apply for credit or a mortgage you want this number to be as low as possible. Lenders have very stringent debt to income ratio polices in place to protect themselves from borrower's who could possibly default on any loan. Obviously, the less debt you have means the lower your ratio and the higher chance of getting a loan at a low interest rate.

Most lenders use a ratio chart and other financial tools to determine several aspects of a loan. For instance, if you have a low credit ratio and a higher credit score you will get a good interest rate on your loan. This means you will save hundreds of dollars just in interest alone over the term of the loan. Although, most lenders prefer the low ratio and high credit score, the average ratios are around 30 to 42 percent. This in return would have a considerable impact on your interest rate and will end up costing you more over the term of the loan.

2

Example:

Healthy Debt to Income Ratio To Carry 36% or less
Moderate Debt to Income Ratio 37%-42%
High Debt To Income Ratio 43%-49%
Very High Debt To Income Ratio 50% or more

A very healthy Debt to Income ratio to carry is 36% or less. The majority of lenders will look very favorable on loaning you money and at a good interest rate.

A moderate Debt to Income Ratio is not bad and most lenders will loan you money just at a higher interest rate. However, you need to look at your debt seriously and pay down your current obligations before taking on anymore finical burdens.

A high Debt to Income Ratio should give you a red flag. You are in financial dilemma and you must take immediate action before its too late. No lender will loan you money.

The final Debt to Income Ratio is very unfavorable. If your Debt to Income Ratio is exceeding the 50% mark you need to seek professional help immediately. By not getting your debt down could mean you are in a financial melt down and even possibly headed for bankruptcy.

Now, that you understand Debt to Income Ratio, you may want to know just how to track all of your debit and income. There are many FREE tools available on the Internet to help you track and monitor your debt. You can use www.mint.com or www.quicken.com both of these sites have excellent financial tools and resources.

Chapter 2

How To Determine Your Net Worth

 The first chapter focused on finding your Debt to Income Ratio. In this chapter we will look at determining your total current net worth. What is Net Worth? Net Worth is two factors, one is your total assets, the other is your total liabilities. Your assets is what is owned or if you sold everything of value the total dollar amount of the items. Your liabilities are what is owed to creditors.

 A net worth statement is important to you and your family. It shows several important factors such as your financial progress that you are making. It can also give you a very good indication of your retirement and financial goals. It provides you with a way to insure that you have enough insurance coverage (Home & Life) in case your siblings have to make it without you. Other aspects include keeping on track with your financial goals and plan for any changes in your assets and liabilities.

Assets consist of three basic types:

1) Current Assets: These are actual cash on hand or items that can be sold quickly for cash. Also included are savings and money market accounts.

2) Fixed Assets: This asset is more for tangible items that could not be sold quickly such as automobiles and home.

3) Differed Assets: This is accounts such as IRA, 401K etc... If you cashed these out then you would pay a high penalty.

Liabilities consist of two types:

1. Current Liabilities: These are in the form of being paid within the current 12 month period.

2. Long Term Liabilities: Which extend for a longer period of time greater than 12 months.

Below I have included a Net Worth Worksheet for you to use. Simply fill out all the required information in each field that directly applies to you.

Net Worth Sheet	As of _____ (date)
Assets	
Cash on Hand	$
Checking Account	$
Savings Account	$
Certificates	$
Money Owed You	$
Tax Refund Due	$
Cash Value-Life Ins.	$
Stocks/Bonds	$
Mutual Fund Shares	$
Other	$
Other	$
Other	$
Other	$
Total Current Assets	$
Fixed Assets	
Automobiles	$
Home	$
Personal Property	$
Other	$
Other	$
Other	$
Total Fixed Assets	$

Deferred Assets	
Retirement Plan	$
I.R.A.	$
Other	$
Other	$
Other	$
Other	$
Total Deferred Assets	$

Now take the totals of each type of asset and write the figures in the corresponding boxes below. Then simply total them, this will be your total over all assets.

Total Of All Assets	
Total Current Assets	$
Total Fixed Assets	$
Total Deferred Assets	$
Total Assets	$

Liabilities	
Current & Long Term Liabilities	
Auto Loan	$
Installment Debt	$
Personal Loan	$
Charge Accounts	$
Credit Cards	$
Mortgage Loan	$
Insurance Due	$
Taxes Due	$
Other	$
Other	$
Other	$
Other	$
Other	$
Total Current Liabilities	$

To find your personal Net Worth, enter in the form below the over all Total of your Assets. In the second box enter the Total Current Liabilities. Then subtract the liabilities from the total assets and write the figure in the box labeled Total Net Worth.

Total Assets	$
Total Current Liabilities	$
Total Net Worth	$

The Federal Reserve System states, the average American household has a net worth equal to five times its debt load. Your Net Worth should keep increasing as you get older. It is recommended that you make a net worth statement once a year. Make sure you always keep a copy of each year. This will help you make better informed decisions when it comes to financial issues in the future.

Chapter 3

Setting Up A Monthly Budget

Creating a plan to pay off your debt is not complicated. There are many ways to do this, but lets stick to a very straight forward approach. In the previous chapter you learned a simple and basic step of finding your current Debt to Income Ratio. Now that you have completed your Debt To Income Ratio worksheet put this aside for Chapter 4

First, lets take a close look at setting up a personal budget. You may ask, why do I need a budget ? Simple, this will help you personally track all your expenses and income. It will help you understand how you can take the extra money you saved during the month, not spent on bills, and pay down your debt. Remember, a budget is a tool to help you understand how to effectively manage debt and income.

To set up a budget on your computer you will need to use software. Here are a few that are FREE, www.pearbudget.com , www.billster.net, www.mint.com, www.quicken.com .

There are several FREE budget templates for excel / open office that will help you get started. You can do a search on the Internet for Free Budget Templates. Or you can go to Micro Soft ® website and download the free financial templates they have.

Take your time and review each of the above items and select one that you will fill comfortable with and sign up for the services or download the template. Or you can use the one provided in this book.

The next step to setting up a budget is to see just how long it will take you to pay off your debts. There is many types of on line calculators to help you achieve this step. Here is one such **FREE DEBT CALCULATOR** you can use. Just download the file and it can be used on Micro Soft Excel® or Open Office ®.

Now that you have the necessary tools that you will need to properly develop your budget, lets get started. No matter how hard we try for the majority of people they do not like the word <u>budget</u>. This word simply scares people in general. In order for you to properly control your finances it is a necessary requirement.

Setting up your budget involves several steps.

1) <u>No what your expenses are:</u>

You already have your basic expenses listed from the work sheet. Now all you need is to gather the remainder of your receipts for food etc.. If you do not have the receipts then use your checkbook or on line bank statement to gather the remaining information.

2) <u>Create categories for your expenses:</u>

I would highly recommend using one of the free spreadsheet templates or use the one provided below. You have the ability to alter these to fit your specific needs. The most important factor in creating your categories is to cover all of your expenses. Make sure you are saving at least <u>15%</u> of your income back each time you get paid. Saving for unexpected emergencies is a must for your budget to work.

3) <u>Add up your expenses:</u>

Now that you have entered all of your expenses, add up each column and total your expenditures at the bottom. This will show you the total of expenditures for the month to date. You can use the budget worksheet provided at the end of this chapter as a guide.

4) <u>Add up your income:</u>

Now you will need to add up all of the income you have listed at the top of the budget worksheet. Once you have a total then transfer the figure to the bottom of the monthly budget worksheet and do the math.

5) <u>Is your budget Balanced:</u>

You can see the differences between your monthly income and the monthly bills. If you have a positive outcome with money left over then you achieved a positive or balanced budget. If your budget turns out to be negative you will need to review your expenditures and make cuts to balance your budget.

Monthly Budget
Fill out all fields that pertain to your finances and leave the rest blank
Remember: this is for your monthly budget not yearly
Any items that are in question you will need to estimate the expense/income
Very Important: Make sure you are properly adding and subtracting your expenses and income
Always use a calculator to add and subtract your work sheet. Use scrap paper if necessary.

Monthly Income	
Income #1 (remember Use your Net Income Only After Taxes)	+$
Income #2 (remember Use your Net Income Only After Taxes)	+$
Income #3 (remember Use your Net Income Only After Taxes)	+$
Income #4 (remember Use your Net Income Only After Taxes)	+$
Net Monthly Income From Pay Checks(Total of All Pay Checks)	=$
If you have a savings/401k/investments (Subtract From Total)	-$
Adjusted Net Monthly Income	=$
NOTE: If you receive any of the following you will need to add it as income.	
AFDC/ TANF (The total you receive on a monthly basis)	+$
Food Stamps (The total you receive on a monthly basis)	+$
Social Security/SSI (The total you receive on a monthly basis)	+$
Any Other Income	+$
Child Support (Add If You Receive-Subtract if you Pay)	-/+$
Alimony (Add If You Receive-Subtract if you Pay)	-/+$
Total Adjusted Monthly Income	=$

Note: Carry the above Total Adjusted Monthly Income to this page of this worksheet.

Housing Expenses			
Total Adjusted Monthly Income (FROM PAGE 1)			+$
Rent or Mortgage Payment (Monthly)	+	$	
Second Mortgage/Home Equity Line	+	$	
Electricity	+	$	
Heating Oil/Gas/Propane	+	$	
Water	+	$	
Sewer	+	$	
Garbage/Recycling Pickup	+	$	
Internet	+	$	
Home Phone	+	$	
Home Repairs (This Should be part of your savings)	+	$	
Maintenance (Cleaning,Pest Control, Lawn etc...)	+	$	
Insurance (Home Owners, Flood etc...)	+	$	
Taxes (Property, etc...)	+	$	
Total Housing Cost	+	$	-$
Monthly Available Income For Other Expenses			$

Automobile & Transportation Expenses			
Monthly Available Income For Other Expenses			$
Gas	+	$	
Insurance	+	$	
Automobile Loan #1	+	$	
Automobile Loan #2	+	$	
Automobile Loan #3	+	$	
Repairs (This Should be part of your savings)	+	$	
Maintenance (Car wash, Oil Changes, etc...)	+	$	
Other Transportation (Bus,Taxi,Train,Carpool,etc..)	+	$	
Total Car & Transportation Expenses	=	$	-$
Monthly Available Income For Other Expenses			$

Note: Carry the above Total Adjusted Monthly Income to page three of this worksheet.

Credit Card & Loan Debt			
Monthly Available Income For Other Expenses			$
Creditor Name	Current Balance	Payment	Balance
#1_____	+$( )	-$	+$
#2_____	+$( )	-$	+$
#3_____	+$( )	-$	+$
#4_____	+$( )	-$	+$
#5_____	+$( )	-$	+$
#6_____	+$( )	-$	+$
#7_____	+$( )	-$	+$
#8_____	+$( )	-$	+$
#9_____	+$( )	-$	+$
#10_____	+$( )	-$	+$
Total Credit Card & Loan Debt		-$	
Monthly Available Income For Other Expenses			$

Dependent Expenses (Child)		
Monthly Available Income For Other Expenses		$
Child Care (Daycare, etc...)	-	$
College Fund	-	$
Diapers	-	$
Baby-Sitting	-	$
School Tuition	-	$
School Supplies & Related Expenses (uniforms, etc)	-	$
Activity Lessons (Band, Piano,Gymnastics, etc..)	-	$
Allowance/ Lunch Money	-	$
Other Child expenses	-	$
Total Dependent Expenses	-	$
Monthly Available Income For Other Expenses		$

Note: Carry the above Total Adjusted Monthly Income to this page of this worksheet.

General Expenditures		
Monthly Available Income For Other Expenses	██████	$
Health Insurance (If Not Paid By Employer) -	$	
Life Insurance (If Not Paid By Employer) -	$	
Groceries -	$	
Dining Out -	$	
Cell Phone or Pager -	$	
Charitable Contributions (Church,Donations, etc..) -	$	
Pet Care (Food, Vet Bills, etc...) -	$	
Clothing (Include Cleaners,Laundry,Uniforms, etc.) -	$	
Hair & Nail Care -	$	
Prescriptions (Not Covered by Insurance) -	$	
Medical Bills (Deductibles, Office Visits, etc..) -	$	
Computer (Printer, Paper, Ink, etc...) -	$	
Postal Supplies (Postage,Stamps, etc..) -	$	
Newspaper & Magazine Subscriptions	$	
Gifts (Birthday,Anniversary,Wedding, etc..) -	$	
Health Club Dues -	$	
Other Club Dues -	$	
Hobbies -	$	
Cigarettes, Alcohol etc.... -	$	
Other Entertainment (Movies,Video, Vacation) -	$	
Other -	$	
Total Of General Expenditures -	$	
Monthly Remaining Income (What Is Left)	+/-	$

 The next section, of the Budget Worksheet listed below, requires all the figures from above worksheets and helps you consolidate them into one final worksheet. From here you will be able to determine your expenses to income and your net worth.

Total Of All Monthly Expenses	
Total Housing Expenditures	$
Total Car & Transportation Expenditures	$
Total Credit & Loan Expenditures	$
Total Dependent Expenditures	$
Total General Expenditures	$
Total Of All Expenditures	$

Total Available Income		$
Total Surplus (Carried Forward From Previous Month)	+	$
Total Shortage (Carried Forward From Previous Month)	-	$
Total Of All Expenditures	-	$
Total Monthly Surplus Or Shortage (Whats Left)		$

 This concludes the monthly budget worksheet. Depending on your total net income and the number of expenses you have over a period of a month will determine if you have a surplus of money. Or, if you need to look at cutting back on your expenditures to balance your budget.

 You will need to look at expenses in your General Expenditures category first and start making cuts here to begin.

 In the next chapter we will discuss how to use this budget to effectively create a plan not only to pay down your debt faster, but further, help show you how to trim your current budget to achieve a well balanced budget.

Chapter 4

Creating A Plan To Pay Off Debt

By now you have learned how to figure your own debt to income ratio as stated in Chapter 1. You have learned how to effective use a budget to track all of your income and expenditures. The next step is to determine how you will pay off your debt. Creating a plan that is not only solid but what works best for you is important. There are many methods to paying off debt and we will discuss the most effective ways in this chapter.

The first step, know that you must be aggressive in paying down your debt. Staying focused on saving every dollar you can within your budget. By sticking to your plan you will avoid extra fees and interest which in return saves you money. Which equates to you paying less each month.

Secondly, be realistic, trying to overcome a large debt fast can cause your budget to shrink and you will end up short every month. You will have to sacrifice in order to get a handle on your overall debt. Don't be shy to cut out as much General Debt as you can, this allows you to concentrate a larger amount of income to paying off your debt.

Next you must ask yourself how do I want to pay this debt down ? Which cards, loans etc.. do I tackle first? Again, there is no right or wrong way to do this, however, the top two methods commonly used are highest interest rate loans and cards first and lowest amount owed.

To make your debt plan effective you may want to use this

FREE DEBIT CALCULATOR .

Simply download the software and install it over Micro Soft Excel ® or Open Office ®. Then input the data into the fields as requested and calculate the amount of months it will take you to pay off your debt.

Once you have determined the approach you will take, then use a piece of paper or the sheet below to organize your debt and list each card, loan etc.. you want to pay off in descending order.

Provided below are forms to use in assisting you on prioritize your debt.

Debt Pay Off Plan Worksheet

Use this worksheet to make your get-out-of-debt plan. List your debts in the order you plan to pay them off either by highest interest rate or lowest balance. Then, in the "Pay Off Payment" column, put the monthly payment you're going to send to the focus account - the account you're working to pay off first. When you've paid off one credit card, mark it off the list and update the "Pay Off Payment" column for the next credit card. Once you have successfully paid off the first card. Use the money that was used to pay off the first debt and apply the amount that is now free from the first card and pay it on the second card plus the minimum payment due on the second card.

Put the amount that you can afford in addition to your budget here $_____

Credit Card	Balance	Rate	Minimum Payment	Pay Off Payment

Debt Pay Off Tracking Worksheet

Use this worksheet to track your progress paying off a credit card or loan. Update as you make payments to see the great progress you're making.

Account#_____   Account#_____

Date	Payment	New Balance	Date	Payment	New Balance

Account#_____   Account#_____

Date	Payment	New Balance	Date	Payment	New Balance

Time to put your new debt plan into action. For ease of use , let us say you have determined you can afford to spend an extra $200.00 a month to be applied toward your debt. And you have opted to start paying your highest amount owed (credit card/Loan) first. For example you owe $1000.00 dollars to your Visa credit card and your minimum monthly payment is $40.00. You would pay the regular monthly payment of $40.00 plus add the extra $200.00 to it for a total of $240.00 payment. Your balance would now only be $760.00 plus the interest for the next month. By repeating this step until this is paid in full will result in paying this debt in full in a matter of a short span instead of years.

Your second debt owed is $850.00 and your monthly payment is around $36.00 monthly. The money that was used to pay off your first card is now free to pay on your next debt. Remember, you were paying a minimum of $40.00 on the first debt monthly. Your monthly contribution to your debt fund is $200.00 for a total of $240.00 now that the first debt has now been payed. The second debt you will pay the minimum payment of $36.00 plus the $240.00 you now have in your debt fund for a total of $306.00 to be paid for that month. This would now leave a balance of only $544.00. To continue just keep repeating this formula until your debt is settled and you become totally debt free.

This method above is termed Debt Snowballing and you must admit it will get you and your family out of debt quicker.

Another method of paying your debt down is to start with the smallest debt you have first. And continue working your way to the largest debt you have. The same factors still would apply you merely start with the smallest debt and work up to the largest debt.

Now that you have a overview of how to pay your debt down, don't forget one of the most important factors of your plan. I mentioned that you need to put back 15% for your savings. Again, don't overlook this factor. Setting aside money for home repairs, car repairs, etc... is a smart way to keep your budget on track. The unexpected will happen, don't be shy to save money for a rainy day. Sure, you can take out the credit card and pay for these unforeseen expenses. But, consider what you are doing with your budget when you make these charges when you could and should have used cash from your savings to pay for this expense.

Chapter 5

Debt vs. Credit

What does reducing or eliminating debt have to do with my credit ? Most people are not aware of how debt affects your credit and credit score. Paying your debt in full will reflect on credit in a critical way. Reducing your debt will almost assure you of not only getting a better rate on future loans but you would qualify for larger amounts. Mortgages can be refinanced to save you hundreds of dollars each year. In return, this allows you to continue to pay your debt down faster.

You must understand how a credit score of 760 will get you a lower interest rate than a score of 640. Myfico.com has more information on the importance of your credit scores.

There are many factors that are involved in your credit score. One of the most important factors is paying your bills on time. Being late on payments will reflect on your overall credit and score. One example of this would be paying a auto loan late. This will cost you 40 to 60 points off your score. Once you have gone late it will take you 6 months to a year of making your payments on time for the creditor to even consider removing this from your credit file. It is much easier setting up bill payment reminders to help you get your payments in before the due date.

As you work through your budget and you begin to pay off your credit cards make sure you **DO NOT CLOSE THE ACCOUNTS**. If you close the account the creditor will show it (paid in full / agreed) but will enter on your report (consumer requested closed account). This will not help you in any way. In fact, this is more of a negative item than a positive. By placing the card away in a safe place would be a better solution. Remember the balance on the account may reflect a 0 balance. However, the account is still active and it continues to show a excellent payment history. The other factor is length of time account is open. Keeping the account in a active status will assure you of a solid credit history.

Chapter 6

Debt Consolidation

In this chapter I will discuss Debt Consolidation. To most, this would seem to be a great way to not only get out of debt but reduce the amounts of monthly payments. Yes, this will reduce the interest rate you are paying over the term of the loan. However, what these Debt Consolidation company's fail to tell you is your overall term on the loan has been extended. The truth is you will pay a smaller amount of money on your debt each month. But the term in which you just signed, has been extended for 12 to 24 months.

Now lets do the math, if you have a loan of $4000.00 for 2 years at a rate of 12% interest and another loan of $6000.00 for 4 years at 10% interest. The loan for $4000.00 will cost you $188.00 dollars a month. The second loan of $6000.00 would cost you $152.00 a month.

Example:

Loan Amount	Interest Rate	Term	Payment
$4000.00	12%	24 months	$188.00
$6000.00	10%	48 months	$152.00

Take this a step further. On the first loan of $4000.00 dollars your payment is $188.00 monthly. To find out overall what you are paying in interest multiply the monthly payment of $188.00 x 24 =$4512.00 this will be your total pay back of the loan. The lender will make $512.00 of interest by loaning you the $4000.00. The second loan you have is calculated the same way. Monthly payment of $152.00 x 48=$7296.00 the lender will make $1296.00 on this loan. Both loans combined the interest alone is $1808.00. Nice chunk of change for borrowing $10,000.00 dollars.

A debt consolidation company would call the lender(s) and negotiate a lower payment on your behalf.

This would include lowering you payments and possibly your interest rates. Lets take this scenario, the Debt Consolidation company makes a deal with your lender to reduce your payments and interest rate.

The loans are then restructured to reduce the interest rate and payments. The Debt Consolidation company has now rolled this into one monthly payment of $180.26. You are now saving $159.74 monthly. Wow!!! But wait, the real kicker is they were able to reduce your interest rate to 9%. And, what they fail to tell you is that these loans just got extended from a 2yr/4yr loan to a 6 year loan. Now on the original loans you first took out for $4000.00 and $6000.00, the interest combined was $1808.00 total. The new loan is now been extended to six years and even though you are paying less on a monthly payment, you are paying a larger amount of interest. In fact, the term of the new loan will put the interest at $2978.72. Now you are paying a large amount of interest for nothing. The new, longer term interest is now $2978.72 minus the original interest of $1808.00, equal a total additional cost to you of $1170.72 over the term of the loan.

One of the most important factors is, they are making money off of each client they have, including you, and face it, its just business. One of the most disturbing truths of Debt Consolidation is that the success rate is only around 22%. Which means that 78% of the people who choose to consolidate there debts end up back in debt because they are not living on a budget. They simply cannot stop buying and using money usefully. I can not stress enough how important it is to not only budget your money but make sure you are saving enough to cover unforeseen expenses.